Love Listens:
Learning to Hear Again

A Parable of Recovered Love

Love Listens:

Learning to Hear Again

A Parable of Recovered Love

By Dr Chuck Carrington

CONNECT
BOOKS

This is a nonfiction work. However, certain sections have been lightly fictionalized or dramatized for illustrative purposes. Any resemblance to actual persons, living or deceased, is purely coincidental.

CONNECT
BOOKS

Connect Books
USA
PO BOX 903 Wakefield VA. USA 23888

Scripture quotations marked (NIV) are taken from the Holy Bible, New International Version®, NIV®. Copyright © 1973, 1978, 1984, 2011 by Biblica, Inc.™

Scripture quotations marked (ESV) are from The Holy Bible, English Standard Version®, copyright © 2001 by Crossway Bibles, a publishing ministry of Good News Publishers.

Occasional references are made to the KJV, which is in the public domain.

Why I Wrote This Book

As a Christian counselor, I've spent decades sitting with couples who long to be closer, but don't know how to cross the emotional distance between them. They love each other—but their words miss the mark. One feels invisible. The other feels inadequate. And they both retreat into silence, resentment, or exhaustion.

This little book was born out of those sacred conversations.

Rather than offer advice in lecture form, I wanted to tell a story. A story that feels familiar. A story that helps you see your own marriage with new eyes—not through the lens of blame, but through the lens of empathy.

If you're holding this book, chances are you're tired of trying to fix your marriage with more words. That's good.

Because love doesn't start with talking—it starts with listening.

This parable is for the wife who feels unseen. And the husband who feels like he's always failing. It's for anyone who's ever wondered, "Why can't we hear each other anymore?"

My hope is that this story gives you a quiet place to begin again.

And maybe... the courage to ask for help.

—Dr. Chuck Carrington

Session One:
The Noise Between Us

The chairs were slightly angled toward each other—just enough to invite connection, but not enough to force it. *The Counselor* had arranged them that way on purpose. In the silence before the couple entered, he adjusted one slightly, not because it was off, but because they were. And he knew—by week's end—he'd need that chair to be ready.

The door swung open with the sound of two people trying not to finish an argument.

"I'm just saying, if you'd stop interrupting me—"

"—If you'd actually listen, you wouldn't think I was interrupting."

4 Dr Chuck Carrington

Aaron and Marissa sat down without looking at each other. Arms crossed. Shoulders tense. Breath shallow.

The Counselor didn't rush to fill the space. He just looked at them, slowly, kindly. Like someone listening to more than words.

"Welcome," he said, after the silence had done its work. "Tell me: in the conversation you just had—did either of you feel heard?"

Marissa blinked.

Aaron shifted. "No," they said, almost at the same time.

He smiled gently, pulling a manila folder from the side table. "This is the first of four files I'll give you. You won't finish them all at once. But if you open them with humility, they will open something in you."

He handed the folder to Marissa. In neat script on the tab, it read:

Attending is Not Agreeing, It's Being Present.

She looked at Aaron, then opened the folder.

Inside was a single sentence:

> **To attend is to offer your presence, not your position.**

She looked up. "So... we're not here to solve things?"

"Not yet," *The Counselor* replied. "You're here to learn how to hear. Most couples never stop talking long enough to notice they stopped listening years ago."

Aaron folded his hands, then unfolded them. "So... what do we do?"

The Counselor stood and moved to the white shelf behind him. From it, he pulled a clear plastic case containing a deck of laminated cards.

He handed them to Aaron. "These are feeling cards. Next week, we'll use them. But for now, just take them home. Skim through them. And tonight, when Marissa speaks—don't try to fix anything. Don't judge it. Just listen. Then name two feelings you heard."

Aaron looked down at the cards. Abandoned. Invisible. Defensive. Hopeful.

He swallowed. "That's... gonna be harder than it sounds."

"Most things worth learning are," said The Counselor.

Marissa gave a small, unexpected smile. The first since they walked in.

The Counselor stood, signaling the close of their time. "Your ears can't hear what your heart refuses to open. Start there. Come back next week ready to attend."

They left quietly. Still not fixed. Still unsure. But something was different.

This time, they left *together*.

Session Two:
Listen With the Eyes First

When Aaron and Marissa returned, they were quieter—but in a different way. Not silent out of anger. More like people carrying something fragile they didn't want to drop.

They sat down more slowly this time. No sharp words. Just an awkward glance, then stillness.

The Counselor nodded. "Did you try the exercise with the cards?"

Aaron nodded. "We did. Twice. I listened... I thought I heard anger. But then she told me it was actually sadness."

Marissa added gently, "It was easier for me to say what I felt when I saw the words. And it was easier to believe he was listening—because he didn't jump in."

The Counselor smiled. He reached for the second manila folder.

Listen With You Eyes.

"Before you open that," he said, "I want to try something."

He took the feeling cards and shuffled them, then handed the stack to Marissa.

"I want you to think of a moment this week that stirred something in you—pleasant or painful. Don't say what happened. Just hold the cards that describe how you felt."

She took a moment, then pulled out *Unseen*, *Alone*, and *Hurt*.

The Counselor turned to Aaron. "Now, without knowing the story—what are your eyes telling you about her face?"

Aaron looked at her. Really looked. He saw the curve in her brow, the damp shimmer in her lashes.

"She's... tired. And afraid I'll miss it again."

Marissa's eyes filled. "That's the first time you've seen me in a long time."

The Counselor let the moment settle, then handed Aaron the folder.

Inside it read:

> **Empathy is not the act of knowing what to say. It is the courage to see without shrinking away.**

"When you listen with your eyes," he explained, "you begin to feel with them too. The face reveals what words conceal."

Marissa reached for Aaron's hand. He let her.

"Next time," the Counselor said, "we'll talk about the wounds that form when presence is missing. For now, keep practicing. Look longer. Listen softer."

They left differently this time.

Marissa looked back and smiled.

And Aaron noticed.

Session Three:
The Wound You Didn't See

The rain had started just before their session. It traced silver lines down the window as the couple sat in silence. Marissa held a tissue she hadn't used yet. Aaron's jaw flexed like he wanted to speak—but didn't know where to begin.

The Counselor glanced toward the rain. "It's quiet outside today. Feels like it wants us to go deeper."

He opened a drawer and took out the third manila folder.

The Wound You Did Not See

He didn't hand it over. Not yet.

Instead, he asked gently, "Marissa, would you be willing to tell Aaron about a moment—not recent, maybe even months ago—when you felt invisible? A time when you needed him to *see* you, and he didn't."

She nodded, her eyes already wet. "There was a night... maybe six months ago. I don't even know if you remember it. I was in the kitchen, crying—quietly. You were on the couch watching a game. I had just gotten off the phone with my sister. She'd told me her cancer came back."

Aaron looked stunned.

"I didn't say anything because I wanted to see if you'd notice. I waited for you to turn around. To check on me. But you didn't. And I felt so... abandoned." She choked on the word.

Aaron sat frozen, the memory flickering in like a film reel he hadn't known existed. "I didn't know. I—I didn't hear you crying."

"That's just it," she whispered. "It wasn't about the volume. It was about the silence. I was hurting right next to you, and you didn't see it."

The Counselor leaned forward slightly. "That moment created something between you—a silence with weight. That's what we call an empathic wound."

Aaron swallowed hard. "I didn't mean to hurt you. I would've helped if I'd known."

The Counselor nodded. "Most empathic wounds aren't intentional. They're not about what we *did*. They're about what we *missed*. Absence cuts as deeply as action."

He handed the folder to Aaron now.

Inside, a single phrase:

> **Empathic wounds form not from what was said—but from what wasn't attended to.**

Aaron held the paper like it might burn. "I've done that more than once, haven't I?"

Marissa didn't answer with words. Just tears.

"I want to do better," he said, voice low. "I just don't know how to go back and fix that."

"You don't," the Counselor said. "But you *do* repair it."

Aaron looked up.

"Next time," the Counselor continued, "we'll walk through how to make empathic repairs. For now, sit with this truth: your absence hurt her. And your presence, now, can begin to heal what your silence once broke."

The room stayed quiet for a long time. Not the sharp silence of defensiveness, but the soft kind that follows honesty.

When they stood to leave, Aaron paused before the door. "Do I say sorry now? Or... later?"

The Counselor smiled. "Start with your eyes. Let her see that you see."

And this time, he did.

Session Four:
The Repair

Marissa sat quietly, hands folded in her lap. Aaron looked different this week—tired, but not heavy. Like someone who had finally stopped carrying a lie.

The Counselor gave them a moment before beginning. "What stayed with you from last week?"

Aaron was the first to speak. "That I missed her pain... more than once. It's been on my mind every day. I see her differently now. And it's... sobering."

Marissa nodded slowly. "He's been quieter. But present. I think I'm still waiting to believe it's real."

The Counselor gave a thoughtful nod, then reached into his drawer and handed them the fourth folder.

Repair is Greater than Regrets.

Inside, they read:

> **You can't erase a wound. But you can help it heal.**

Aaron read it twice, then looked up. "So how? I want to make it right—but I don't want to make it worse."

The Counselor leaned forward. "That's the right instinct. A true repair doesn't come from pressure. It comes from presence, patience, and humility. I'll guide you through it. One step at a time."

He pulled a card from his desk. On it were five short phrases:

1. Listen Closely
2. Acknowledge the Hurt
3. Take Responsibility
4. Offer a Sincere Apology
5. Make Amends

He handed it to Aaron.

Aaron took a breath. "Can I try now?"

The Counselor nodded.

Aaron turned to Marissa. His voice was low but steady. "I hear now how alone you've felt. Especially that night in the kitchen. I wasn't there. I didn't see you. And I know that hurt you deeply. I'm sorry. Truly sorry. You didn't deserve that silence from me. I can't go back—but I can be better now. And I want to be."

Marissa's lips trembled. She covered her face briefly, then lowered her hands.

"That's all I've wanted," she whispered. "Not a fix. Just to know that you *see me*—and that it matters to you."

The Counselor smiled warmly. "That, Aaron, was a repair. One that will take time, yes—but it started with a choice.

You didn't defend. You didn't explain it away. You entered the wound... and offered your presence."

Aaron looked at his wife. "I'll keep practicing. Even if I get it wrong sometimes."

Marissa leaned her shoulder toward his. It wasn't everything. But it was something. Something new.

The Counselor stood and walked to the bookshelf. He selected a thin notebook and handed it to them.

On the cover, it read:

Daily Practice: Three Minutes of Listening

"Take this home," he said. "Each day, give each other three minutes. No interruptions. No advice. Just listening for the feeling underneath the words. That's how trust is rebuilt. Three minutes at a time."

They stood, holding the notebook like a fragile seed.

And as they left, it didn't feel like an ending.

It felt like planting something worth waiting for.

Session Five:

Love Learns to Listen

The fifth and final session began not with silence, but with laughter.

Marissa was shaking her head. "He set a timer on his phone for our three-minute talks."

Aaron grinned. "It was either that or I'd start giving advice again without realizing it."

The Counselor smiled at the shift. "Sometimes structure protects what we're still learning to value."

He gestured toward the chairs. "Tell me what's been different this week."

Aaron went first. "I'm realizing that most of the time, I was listening just enough to form a reply. But now, I try to listen until I feel something... not just understand the words."

Marissa nodded. "And when he reflects back my feelings—it's like something unlocks in me. Like I'm finally safe enough to let the rest of it out."

The Counselor leaned back, satisfied. "Then you've learned the hardest part. Listening isn't about hearing the story. It's about holding the heart behind it."

He stood and walked to the cabinet, retrieving a final envelope. This one wasn't manila. It was soft grey, sealed with a silver clasp.

Love Doesn't Lecture, It Listens.

He handed it to them together.

Inside was a single card with a question:

> **What would happen in your marriage if empathy was the starting point for every conversation?**

They read it together. And didn't rush to answer.

Instead, Marissa looked at Aaron. "I think we'd stop trying to win."

Aaron nodded. "And start trying to understand."

The Counselor looked at them with warmth. "Empathy isn't a technique. It's a way of being. You don't practice it to fix each other. You practice it to *find* each other."

They sat for a long while in quiet reflection.

Eventually, *The Counselor* spoke again. "This is where most couples want to arrive at the beginning—closeness, safety, understanding. But you've earned it the right way. One moment of listening at a time."

Aaron exhaled deeply. "It's funny... I used to think love was about saying the right thing. Now I see—it starts by hearing the hard things."

Marissa reached for his hand. "And staying."

As they stood to leave, the Counselor added one final word.

"Keep the cards. Keep the notebook. But more importantly—keep listening. Even when it's inconvenient. Especially when it's emotional. That's when love speaks loudest—by saying nothing at all."

They walked out together, the door clicking quietly behind them.

This time, the silence wasn't empty.

It was full.

Reflection & Practice: Listening with the Heart

This section is designed to help you process the lessons from Aaron and Marissa's journey, and to begin your own. Use these prompts and exercises alone or with your spouse.

1. Reflection Questions (Individual or Couple)

When do you feel most heard in your relationship?

When do you feel least heard?

How do you typically respond when your partner expresses emotion?

Have you ever unintentionally caused an empathic wound? What happened?

What does "being present" mean to you? How can you embody it more fully?

What would change in your relationship if you led with empathy?

2. Listening Practice: The Three-Minute Habit

Try this exercise daily for one week.

Set a timer for 3 minutes.

Partner A speaks, sharing thoughts or feelings from the day.

Partner B listens silently—no interruptions, no fixing, no facial reactions.

After 3 minutes, Partner B reflects back what they heard—especially the *feelings*.

Then switch roles.

Tip: Use feeling cards or a printed emotion wheel to help grow your emotional vocabulary.

3. Repair in Action: The Five-Step Model

When an empathic wound occurs, walk through these five steps together:

1. **Listen Closely** – Let your partner share, uninterrupted.
2. **Acknowledge the Hurt** – Say what you hear, especially the feeling.
3. **Take Responsibility** – Avoid explanations. Own your impact.
4. **Offer a Sincere Apology** – Speak remorse with empathy.
5. **Make Amends** – Ask: "What can I do to begin rebuilding trust?"

4. Spiritual Reflection

Read James 1:19 — "Be quick to listen, slow to speak…"

Meditate on Galatians 6:2 — "Bear one another's burdens…"

Pray together: "Lord, teach us to listen not just with our ears, but with our hearts."

5. Final Encouragement

Listening is not a skill to master—it's a posture to return to again and again. Every time you choose to be present rather than defensive, to reflect rather than react, to attend rather than assume—you practice love.

And love listens.

Part Two

Not many weeks later...

Session Ten:

When the Listener Goes Quiet

Aaron had been doing the work. For the past months, he'd leaned in, stayed present, and listened with growing empathy. Marissa had softened—her smile was returning, her laughter occasionally surfacing like a long-lost friend. But something else had surfaced too: Aaron's silence.

Not the defensive kind—the aching kind.

The Counselor noticed it during their sixth session.

"You're here," he said to Aaron, "but something is missing."

Aaron shifted in his seat. "I guess I'm just tired."

Marissa looked over, concerned. "You've been quieter lately. I thought maybe you were just relieved we were doing better."

Aaron hesitated. "I am. But... I don't know. It's like I've been doing all this listening, and now I realize—there are things I wish someone had asked me, too."

The Counselor nodded. "You've been learning to hear her pain. But now you're beginning to hear your own."

Aaron looked down. "I was raised to suck it up. If I talked about feelings, I got mocked. Even now, I feel like I'd hurt her if I told her how lonely I've been."

Marissa turned fully toward him, her eyes brimming. "You *can* tell me. I didn't know."

Aaron nodded slowly. "That's the point. I didn't know either. Until now."

The Counselor reached into the drawer and handed him a new folder.

When the Strong Go Unseen.

Inside was a single line:

> **Some silences are not strength— they are wounds waiting for welcome.**

He looked at them both. "It's time we talk about how men ache. And how often they ache alone."

Session Eleven:

When Strength Feels Like Silence

The following week, the shift in tone was immediate. Marissa arrived early, anxious. Aaron followed, slower, his shoulders slightly hunched—like a man carrying something sacred but unsure where to set it down.

They sat.

The Counselor didn't speak right away. He let the silence stretch until Aaron finally broke it.

"I've been thinking all week about what I haven't said. What I've buried."

He paused, then added quietly, "And how scared I've been to say it."

Marissa looked over gently, but didn't rush in. She had learned not to fill the space too soon.

"I think," Aaron continued, "I spent so much time trying to be the strong one... I forgot I needed something too. Not just appreciation. Not respect. I needed comfort. I just didn't know how to ask for it."

The Counselor nodded slowly. "And now?"

Aaron looked at Marissa. "Now I wonder if there's room for that. If it's safe for me to feel something without her thinking I'm weak or angry or... broken."

Marissa's eyes softened. "Aaron, I never wanted you to hide. I just didn't know you *needed* anything. You always looked so... okay."

He gave a half-laugh. "That's the problem. I got good at looking okay."

The Counselor leaned forward, voice quiet but steady. "Aaron, would you be willing to try something?"

He nodded.

"I want you to speak from the ache. One sentence at a time. And Marissa— your role is to listen, like he listened to you. Don't explain. Don't soothe. Just reflect what you hear. Use the cards if you need to."

Aaron hesitated, then began. "Sometimes, I feel like I'm only good to you when I'm doing something useful."

Marissa blinked, then reached for a feeling card. *Unseen.* She looked up and said gently, "You feel unseen when I only notice your actions, not your heart."

Aaron nodded, slowly.

Another breath. "Sometimes, I feel like I have to earn peace at home by making sure you're always okay—even when I'm not."

She picked up *Afraid*. "You're afraid of burdening me... so you carry things alone."

His eyes moistened. "Yeah."

They went on for several more minutes, quiet, careful. One feeling at a time. One echo at a time.

When they paused, *The Counselor* offered the next envelope.

When Men Speak, Love Listens Back.

Inside was a card that read:

> **His silence may not mean he has nothing to say. It may mean he doesn't believe it's safe to speak.**

The Counselor spoke softly. "Marissa, empathy isn't just what you needed— it's what he needed too. And now he knows... you're learning to offer it."

She reached over and touched Aaron's hand.

"I want to be a safe place for you, too."

And for the first time in a long time, Aaron nodded—not with effort, but with relief.

Session Twelve:

Making Room for His Pain

The next week, Aaron entered the room with slower breath but more upright shoulders. Marissa walked beside him. Not behind, not ahead—beside.

There was a visible shift in her. The kind that comes when someone realizes empathy isn't about who needs it more—but who offers it next.

The Counselor greeted them and gestured for them to sit.

"Aaron," he began, "last week you took a risk. You let yourself be seen. How did that feel afterward?"

Aaron exhaled. "Raw. But right. Like I'd opened a door that had been locked so long, I forgot it was there."

He looked at Marissa. "And she didn't run. That mattered."

The Counselor nodded. "Marissa, what was that like for you?"

She looked down, then up again. "I was scared at first. Not of what he said—but of what it meant. That I'd been so focused on my pain, I hadn't noticed his. I thought... empathy was about needing it. I didn't know it was also about giving it."

The Counselor smiled gently. "Empathy isn't just medicine for the wounded. It's muscle for the willing."

He stood and offered the next envelope.

His Heart is Not Threat.

Inside, they read together:

> **When a man shares his sorrow, he is not stepping out of strength—he is stepping into trust.**

Aaron blinked, then read it again. "That's... true. I didn't feel weak when I shared. I felt brave."

The Counselor nodded. "That's the paradox. Men have been taught to measure strength by silence. But real strength is the courage to be known."

He turned to Marissa. "Would you be willing to speak that truth back to him?"

She looked at Aaron and took his hand. "Your strength isn't in what you hide. It's in what you trust me enough to share. And I'm here for all of it. Even the hard stuff."

He nodded, visibly moved. "Then I think I can keep sharing."

The Counselor smiled. "That's how relationships grow—not by one person always doing the work, but by both learning to carry what matters to the other."

They sat in quiet for a moment.

Then Marissa whispered, "I think I'm starting to hear you."

Aaron's eyes filled. "That's all I ever wanted."

And that day, the silence between them wasn't filled with pressure or pain.

It was filled with presence.

Session Thirteen:
The Shared Burden

The next session opened with less hesitation. Aaron entered with steadier eyes, and Marissa brought her notebook—already opened to a page with his name written at the top.

The Counselor smiled at the small but telling detail.

"You've both done a lot of inner work," he said. "Now let's talk about what happens next—when your emotional lives begin to overlap."

He handed them the next envelope.

Shared Burdens Build Strong Bridges.

Inside, they read together:

> **Love deepens not when one person is rescued, but when both are carried.**

Aaron looked up. "That feels... right. Like it's not just about who's hurting more, but about learning how to take turns."

The Counselor nodded. "Exactly. Many couples get stuck in emotional triage—always tending to the louder wound. But strength comes when both learn to pause, notice, and respond—even when they're still healing themselves."

Marissa turned to Aaron. "I want to carry what you're still afraid to name. But I need help knowing how."

Aaron smiled gently. "Just don't rush to fix it. I don't need solutions. I need space."

The Counselor added, "And Aaron, your part is learning how to speak your pain without shame. You don't need to prove it deserves airtime. You just need to ask for a hand."

He gave them each a new card with a single shared sentence:

Let's carry this together.

"Use that line this week," he said. "Anytime the old roles try to creep back. Anytime you want to isolate, or when you see your spouse retreating into fear."

Aaron looked at Marissa. "Let's carry this together."

She nodded, with tears. "Always."

They didn't need more words that day.

The work now was not to explain—but to hold.

And they left the session lighter, not
because the weight was gone, but
because they had learned to carry it side
by side.

Session Fourteen: Love That Listens Both Ways

For their final session, Aaron and Marissa sat without fidgeting. No tension in their shoulders. No guarded expressions. Just a quiet steadiness, like two people who had walked through a storm and come out holding hands.

The Counselor welcomed them warmly. "Today we don't open a new envelope. Today, we reflect on the ones you've already opened."

He laid out each folder on the table in front of them:

Attending is Not Agreeing, It's Being Present.

Listen With Your Eyes First.

The Wound You Did Not See.

Repair is Greater than Regrets.

Love Doen't Lecture, it Listens.

When the Strong Go Unseen.

When Strength Feels Like Silence.

His Heart is Not a Threat.

Shared Burdens Build Strong Bridges.

Marissa reached out and gently touched the last one. "That one... changed everything."

Aaron nodded. "They all did. But that's the one where we stopped trying to fix each other and started choosing to stay near the pain—together."

The Counselor smiled. "That is the heart of empathy. It's not about avoiding pain, but about refusing to let each other face it alone."

He handed them one final card— smaller than the others, but heavier with meaning.

Love listens both ways—or it doesn't last.

Aaron read it aloud, then looked at Marissa. "I want to keep practicing that."

She smiled. "So do I."

The Counselor leaned back. "Empathy is now part of your shared language. Not just for conflict. But for daily life. When either of you begins to feel unheard, unheld, unseen—you now have the tools. You have each other."

Aaron said, "It doesn't mean we won't mess up."

"No," the Counselor agreed. "But it means you'll know how to return."

They sat together in quiet agreement. No ceremony. No dramatic goodbye.

Just two people who had learned how to speak less, hear more, and choose each other—again and again.

When they rose to leave, the folders stayed behind.

But the lessons went with them.

Part Three
Keeping it Healthy...

Reflection & Practice: Empathy for Him

This companion section helps couples process the second movement of the journey—the silent pain of men and the mutual listening that transforms both hearts.

1. Reflection Questions for Wives

Have you ever assumed your husband was "fine" because he wasn't expressing emotion?

How do you typically respond when he begins to show vulnerability?

In what ways might you unintentionally make it unsafe for him to share?

What might change if you listened to his unspoken ache with the same tenderness you longed to receive?

2. Reflection Questions for Husbands

Have you been taught to hide pain, grief, or insecurity in order to appear strong?

What has it cost you to stay silent?

What fears surface when you imagine being truly seen?

What would it look like to ask gently for empathy, instead of demanding to be understood?

3. Mutual Listening Exercise

Each partner takes turns answering the question:

"What part of your emotional world feels like it goes unnoticed?"

The listener practices full presence, then reflects back what they heard—especially the feeling.

Use the phrase: "I hear that you felt ___ when that happened, and that matters to me."

Then switch.

4. Anchoring Truths

His silence might be self-protection—
not absence.

Empathy doesn't weaken love—it
protects it.

Love listens both ways—or it doesn't
last.

5. Prayer or Journaling Prompt

Lord, give me ears to hear the pain I've
missed, and the courage to speak the
truth I've hidden. Make our marriage a
safe place for sorrow, healing, and
hope.

Empathic love is not a one-way path.
When both partners become students of
each other's wounds, they become
caretakers of each other's souls.

And in that sacred space—love listens
best.

Reflection & Practice: Empathy for Her

This guide accompanies Part One of the parable 'Love Listens.' It helps couples reflect on the foundational practice of empathic listening—especially the early emotional wounds often carried silently by wives.

1. Reflection Questions for Husbands

When your wife expresses emotion, what is your first instinct—to fix it, defend, or listen?

Have you ever dismissed or minimized her feelings unintentionally?

What messages did you receive growing up about women's emotions?

What would it take for you to become more emotionally present when your wife is hurting?

2. Reflection Questions for Wives

What does it feel like when your spouse truly listens to you?

When do you feel most emotionally abandoned or overlooked?

How do you express emotional pain—and how do you wish he would respond?

Have you given your partner the tools and safety to understand your deeper feelings?

3. Listening Practice: The Three-Minute Method

Set aside three minutes each evening to simply listen to each other.

- One partner speaks, the other listens with full attention.

- After three minutes, the listener reflects back the emotion heard.

- Then switch.

Use this prompt:

"I hear that you felt ___ when that happened. That matters to me."

4. Truths to Anchor the Process

Attending is not agreeing—it's being present.

Empathy is the soil where intimacy grows.

Listening without judgment opens the door to trust.

5. Prayer or Journaling Prompt

Lord, help me become a better listener—not with quick answers, but with quiet compassion. Teach me to attend to the hearts of those I love, and to build safety with my silence as well as my words.

Empathy begins where assumption ends. Listening—not to respond, but to understand—is the first act of love.

And, when one partner listens with their whole heart, the other begins to heal.

The story you just read is more than a parable—it's a mirror. If you found yourself nodding, crying, or whispering *"That's me"*, then you already know this: one-sided love doesn't have to be the end of the story.

The next step is not about working harder or proving your worth. It's about learning to see clearly, love wisely, and live with strength drawn from something deeper than circumstance.

Before Love Can Heal: When Loving Feels One-Sided will walk with you—step by step—through the Four Power Convictions that have changed the lives of thousands of individuals stuck in the same cycle.

You don't have to know how it ends. You just have to take the next faithful step.

You've already shown love. Now, let truth guide it.

Let conviction steady it.

Let healing begin.

Keep going. You're not done yet. The real work—and the real hope— begins here.

Before love can heal... conviction must lead.

Before Love Can Heal:

When Loving Feels One-Sided

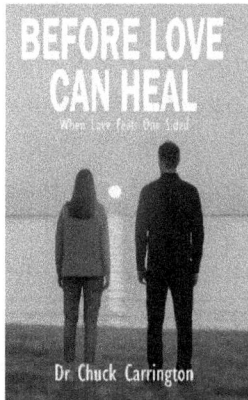

You didn't expect love to feel this lonely.

You've tried to keep the marriage together—giving, praying, hoping. But the more you've poured in, the more distant things have become. Conversations turn into conflict. Your efforts feel invisible. And somewhere along the way, your heart began to wonder: *Is it supposed to be this hard?*

Before Love Can Heal: When Loving Feels One-Sided is written for the one still trying. With warmth, compassion, and deep biblical wisdom, Christian counselor Dr. Chuck Carrington offers a lifeline— not quick fixes or empty clichés, but honest guidance for what to do when love feels heavy, hope feels thin, and you're carrying the weight alone.

This book won't ask you to pretend things are okay. It will invite you to see your story more clearly, understand what's really happening beneath the surface, and take small, Spirit-led steps toward strength, peace, and healing—no matter what your spouse chooses.

You are not alone. You are not crazy. And love that feels one-sided today may still become something redemptive tomorrow.

Hope isn't gone. Healing is still possible. And it begins here.

About the Author

Dr. Chuck Carrington, PhD, EdS, MA, is a seasoned Christian counselor, author, and speaker with over 30 years of experience helping individuals, couples, and families heal from emotional wounds and rediscover the strength of biblical conviction. Known for his clarity, compassion, and unapologetically Christ-centered approach, he has become a trusted voice in the areas of marriage restoration, betrayal trauma recovery, and men's spiritual formation.

Dr. Chuck's counsel is deeply shaped by walking alongside thousands of couples and individuals through seasons of betrayal, heartache, and breakthrough. His voice is that of a wise guide and spiritual shepherd—one who speaks from experience, not distance.

Whether writing, teaching, or counseling, his message remains consistent: real love leads. And it doesn't wait for perfection—it begins when one person chooses conviction over comfort and faithfulness over fairness.

He is the author of several influential works, including *The Renewed Mind*, a guide for men recovering from pornography addiction and rebuilding broken trust; *Bless Your Wife*, a devotional resource for husbands learning to lead with humility and grace; and *Kingship & Character*, a leadership model rooted in the Narnian virtues and the call to biblical manhood. *Letting Love Lead: Samantha's Story* marks a shift in form—offering a fictional parable drawn from decades of real counseling experience. Inspired by the countless men and women who have walked into his office weary from one-sided love, this story gives voice to those who keep showing up, loving faithfully, and wondering if it still matters. Dr. Chuck illustrates the redemptive power of four "Power Convictions"—biblical insights that reposition the heart, and make room for God to work even when love feels unreturned.

A dynamic teacher and mentor, Dr. Chuck serves as Executive Director of a Christian counseling and training center, where he trains the next generation of biblical counselors and coaches. His life's work is rooted in the belief that transformation starts with truth, and that lasting change doesn't come from controlling others—it comes from letting God reshape us from the inside out.

As the founder of Connect Christian Family Counseling and the Relationship Clinic he conducts various training groups, discipleship and leadership groups for Christian men to reclaim integrity, character, and godly purpose in a culture increasingly hostile to biblical masculinity. His teaching blends

scriptural truth with clinically-
informed counseling practices,
offering tools for transformation that
speak to the heart and mind alike.

Whether writing, teaching, or
counseling, his message remains
consistent: real love leads. And it
doesn't wait for perfection—it
begins when one person chooses
conviction over comfort and
faithfulness over fairness.

If You Need Counseling or Help

Dr Chuck offers Christian Faith-Based Counseling and Coaching in trauma, grief and loss, and specializes in men's recovery from porn and cyber-addiction, Betrayal Trauma recovery, and restorative counseling to help heal and recover marriages after betrayal, as well as workshops, online webinars and master classes.

For a consultation via telehealth video, contact Dr Chuck to get more information on how to overcome the damage of betrayal and addiction. Use the website below to sign up for recovery and support groups, or to join Dr Chuck's online psychoeducational programs.

If you are looking for marriage enhancement counseling or coaching, Dr Chuck offers online webinars and forums to help Christian couples explore their marriage, and how it conforms to

God's plan for marriage, to find forgiveness and healing, or to plan for an extraordinary marriage from the outset for engaged couples.

Believers should ask for the Faith-based community discount for the best possible pricing. Free groups include Healing Hearts for women damaged

CONNECT

by betrayal, and Overcomer's Group for men struggling with porn addiction and cyber addiction.

www.connectcounselor.com

**Connect Christian Family
Counseling
757 965-5450**